display a creative curriculum

We are

How many stars can you count?

What other Shapes can you see?

Number Smart

Noel McHugh
gett

Acknowledgements

Creating this book has been a year of hard work, creative thinking and inspiration. We would like to take this opportunity to thank absolutely everyone who has worked tirelessly on any of the displays featured in this book. All the people involved have shown a high level of dedication and a real understanding of what we are trying to achieve.

Noel would like to give special thanks to Head Teacher Fiona Webb and all the staff and children at Glastonbury Thorn School, Milton Keynes for their hard work and dedication. Stephen would like to give special thanks to Head Teacher Linda Nouch, along with the staff and children at Willen Primary School, Milton Keynes for their hard work and patience.

We would both like to say thank you to Head Teacher Mark Thomas and Bev Affleck at Woodland View Primary School, Northampton for their contributions to pages 11, 35 and 68-69. Finally, we would like to say thank you to Zoë Nichols, Kelvin Freeman and Steve Forest for the photo-shoot days.

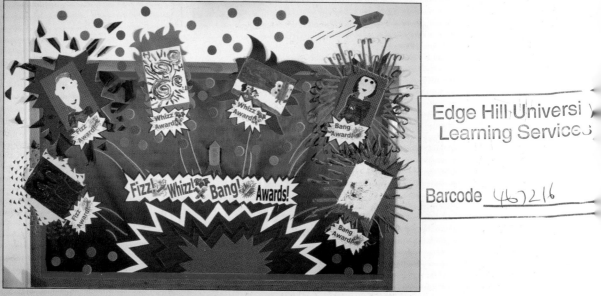

Celebration Display (page 28)

© 2006 Folens on behalf of the authors.

Belair Publications, Apex Business Centre, Boscombe Road, Dunstable, LU5 4RL.
Email: belair@belair-publications.co.uk

Commissioning Editor: Zoë Nichols
Page Layout: Suzanne Ward
Cover Design: Steve West

Editor: Jill Adam
Photography: Kelvin Freeman and Steve Forest

First published in 2006 by Belair Publications.

British Library Cataloguing in Publication ⬛⬛⬛ cation is available from the British Library.

ISBN 0 84191 448 7

Contents

Introduction   4

Whole School Themes
Choosing a School Theme   6
School Reception Area   8
School Hall   10
Music Room   12
Shared Areas   14
Reading Areas   16
Staff Room   18

Classroom Environment
Numeracy Displays   20
Literacy Displays   22
Interactive Displays   24
PSHCE Displays   26
Celebration Displays   28

Learning Environment
How Are You SMART?   30
Learning Styles   32
Mind Mapping   34
Self-evaluation   36

Behaviour and Rewards
Golden Time   38
Reward Activities   40
Behaviour Displays   42
Incentive Displays   44

Communication
School Aims   46
Displays for Visitors   48
School Community Displays   50

Cross-curricular Display
Early Years   52
Literacy Focus   54
Science Focus   56
History Focus   58
RE Focus   62
Geography Focus   64

Themed Weeks
Choosing a Theme   66
Art Theme   68
Theme Days   70
Artist's Day   71

Display Methods   72

Introduction

Displays should be bold, bright, effective and eye-catching as they play an important role in the school environment. Display is a vital tool in developing a creative atmosphere and it is a fantastic way of sharing work and recognising achievements. In addition, displays can be an effective teaching and learning medium, by providing information for the children, and as an interactive feature of the classroom. They are a window into the school; a snapshot of the work, ambiance and learning that takes place in each classroom. Displays are there to represent the school and should be used to communicate with all who work and learn within it, as well as visitors to the building.

The aim of this book is to demonstrate the numerous ways in which you can approach display and to focus on the whole school environment; ensuring creativity is an integral part of everyday school life and features in all areas of the school environment.

The chapters explore different spaces where display can be used. As well as showing children's work, displays can focus on specific areas of the curriculum and support the learning in the classroom. Where possible, displays should be interactive, allowing the children to use them in lessons by responding to the questions they ask. By extending outside traditional areas, displays can become an invaluable tool for everything from helping to maintain school and classroom behaviour to communicating with the wider school community.

Effective displays can be used to build identities in various parts of the school and make use of difficult or unusual spaces. They can be used to give ownership to children who work in shared areas and to welcome people to different year groups as they move through the school. In this way, displays can help build a closer school community and provide an immediate and visual way of communicating.

Creating intricate and expressive displays can seem a large endeavour. However, changing the approach to creating a display can make it a less daunting task. Preparing a display can be a slow process taking several weeks, but can be made less onerous by utilising the entire team from the teacher and teaching assistants through to the children themselves. Displays can start with just a simple board and develop as the teaching and class work progress. Using display in this manner becomes essential when you realise how it can become a focal point for learning.

We believe that through the use of effective planning, and by linking activities across the curriculum, greater scope and resources become available for creating exceptional displays. Cross-curricular themes give children an increased accessibility to a subject, which in turn allows them to develop a greater understanding that is reflected in their work. In writing this book we hope to have produced a valuable resource that is accessible to, and easily used by teachers, head teachers, governors, teaching assistants and parents. Whether you are considering the classroom, the whole school or celebrating work, we aim to help you achieve a creative curriculum.

Noel McHugh and Stephen Springett

Choosing a School Theme

A whole school theme can be used to create a child-friendly and child-oriented environment. Different areas and sections of the school can be joined together under one idea. Within this, individual classes can take on roles and identities that add to the overall theme. With a whole school Jungle Theme each class takes on the name of an animal, for example, the Lions or the Elephants. Open spaces and communal areas can take on identities of their own which are linked to the theme, such as the Jungle Books Reading Zone for the library, shown in the photograph. As the theme is extended throughout the premises the children are constantly reminded that they are members of a whole school community.

Starting Points

1. Staff agree on a selection of themes that would be appropriate for the school.

2. Share these ideas with the children and decide as a school which theme to adopt.

3. Hold a 'themed week' to launch and introduce the new theme and have school-wide art sessions to establish some of the initial visual aspects of the theme.

4. Each class should choose an identity that links to the overall theme and possibly a class motto or song.

5. Rename key areas around the school, such as 'The Clearing' for the hall, 'Jungle Drums' or 'Jungle Beats' for the music room, and 'The Watering-hole' for the canteen.

6. Extend the displays outwards from the classrooms and communal areas into the corridors.

7. Design a large mural featuring the class identities and set it up in a prominent position in the school.

8. Make class symbols from collage materials, such as the lion in the photograph.

9. Display the collage symbols in a main area of the school such as the reception to establish immediate awareness of the theme.

Theme Ideas

- Ocean: focus on the various environments found under the ocean, with classes adopting different sea creatures as their symbols.

- Space: use planets, space stations and space ships to capture the children's imagination.

- Fairy tales: let the classes choose their favourite fairy tale as their identity.

- Airport: use aspects of an airport to rename parts of the school. Classes could be different gates, early years could be renamed Arrivals, and Departures could be the new identity of the top (leaving) class.

- House system: more formal, but by creating a house system within the school, children can be encouraged to think about a new identity across the age groups.

Cross-curricular Links

- **Speaking and listening**: hold a school election to choose the overall theme. Ask children to debate their chosen theme and allow the school to vote for a winner.

- **Literacy/ICT**: research into the chosen theme and produce a newsletter report that can be used to help publicise the activities going on in school.

- **PSHCE**: for a jungle theme produce 'Jungle Vines' as shown here. Each leaf carries a promise about how the children are going to behave and work hard to build a successful jungle. These can be displayed in corridors to enhance the overall effect.

- **Art**: make masks to match each class's chosen identity. These can be used in class assemblies and when representing the school.

- **Drama/Music/PE**: look at, and brainstorm the different characteristics of each class symbol (animals in the jungle, for example - how would they act, walk?). Use music to simulate their movements or choose instruments to represent each symbol. Create a school song or dance involving each class's identity.

School Reception Area

The school reception area sets the first impression of the school. It should act as a window, showing all the different activities that are going on throughout the building. Reception is an excellent space to highlight a school's connection with the wider school community, displaying key information about the school, its staff and future plans. It can be used to communicate with parents and most importantly feature the work that is taking place in the classrooms. The reception area can provide an instant insight into the school, a 'one-stop shop' of information. A 'school gallery' is a successful way of displaying children's work in a stylish and formal manner. Keeping the work up to date is a quick and easy job.

Display

1. Choose a variety of children's work to display, or settle on a main theme. In this example, children's work on Van Gogh was displayed.

2. Select a range of frames in different sizes, in the same style.

3. Mount the work in the frames on the wall in a slightly randomised way (ensure that some frames are placed low down for younger children to see easily). Setting the frames on a strongly coloured wall or background will make them stand out.

4. Create large images that are linked to the work on display and mount them on the wall beneath or behind the frames to create greater interest.

5. Add a title or banner to help explain what the work or lesson was about.

6. To enhance the idea of a gallery, make a signpost as you might see in a museum. It can add fun to the display and serve a practical purpose by showing directions to various parts of the school. In keeping with the art theme, give each year group or area of the school an appropriate name, for example, 'Budding Artists' for early years.

Further Ideas

- Create a display for the sole purpose of welcoming visitors to the school; the school logo could be used as a central image. Here, a collage of jungle animals has been created by the children to represent their class identities.

- Install a glass cabinet that can be used to display 3D work such as clay or DT models. Alternatively, the cabinet could display photographs of the staff and governors. (It will create a greater insight into the school if these photos are 'action' shots of the staff engaged in activities rather than a composed studio portrait.)

- Provide plants, seating and maybe background music to give a welcoming and safe environment where people will be encouraged to take their time to look around.

- A computer could be set up to show the school website, or a PowerPoint display could continually show images of children's work and pictures from around the school or school events.

- Positive remarks from the visitors' log book or suggestion book can be used to enhance the area. A simple idea is to word process comments you want to share onto coloured paper and stick them on gold coloured stars to hang from the ceiling in the reception area.

School Hall

Displays in the school hall are ideal for reaching every member of the school community, through assemblies, concerts and at break times. To continue the idea of an interactive environment these displays need, where possible, to be interactive across all age groups. An information or school council display is ideal for this space as it will be relevant to everyone. Such generic displays should link in with the whole school theme as the content itself may not be eye-catching in the way that topic or class based work is. A lively image from the school theme can draw people to the display where they could find important information.

Display

1. Choose an image that links with the whole school theme to provide a backdrop for the display – in this case, jungle animals.

2. Hang a large sheet of paper to cover the entire main display board.

3. Use an overhead projector to project an enlarged image onto the board and draw around the outline. (Make sure the outline 'bursts' the borders of the display board.)

4. Once the outline is cut out, use paint to create the main features of the chosen image.

5. For the school council display, the question of the week is placed in the speech bubble. Children drop their answers into the boxes stapled to the front of the display.

6. Pose questions for the whole school community to consider on issues that the school council thinks are relevant. Maintain a space on the display where the results from previous surveys can be given.

7. Sharing assemblies, where a class of children 'share' their work with the rest of the school, are popular. An alternative to this is for teachers to share their learning processes. Showing children that teachers have to work hard to learn a new skill is a great way to encourage their own learning. In this example, (left), a teacher was learning to play the cornet. She showed the results of her learning in a weekly assembly and displayed a diary of her progress for the children to read.

Further Ideas

- Make an assembly display where current and future assembly themes can be introduced. This can help generate interest in the assembly, especially if pictures of participants become part of the display each week. It is possible to turn the maintenance and upkeep of the board over to the children taking part in the assembly.

- If you have chosen a central theme for the school you could use the hall space to display large pieces of artwork linked to the theme. A class could work with a local artist to produce a communal piece of work. Here, (left), an artist has collaborated with a class on the theme of seasons to produce a huge mosaic.

- Additional artwork on the theme can be produced by other classes and displayed alongside the artist's work. For example, children could make clay tiles to represent the theme. These could be mounted and framed together, as shown below.

- Certificates of children's achievements can form a focal point for the school hall. Having their success diplayed in such a prominent position is something the children can be proud of.

- When displaying artwork in the hall invite children from different classes to try their hand at the skill or style of the work on display. Run a competition, with the best entries displayed alongside the current class's work.

- Create a cross-curriculum board where samples of work are displayed from each subject and from every class. This can be updated regularly and will provide a great insight into the work that each class is doing.

Music Room

The music room in a school offers tremendous access to the whole school community. The room will be visited by most classes during the week and therefore is an ideal place to display work and catch children's interest in music and other subjects. Displays could be based on musical notes and instruments. To create an interactive environment the notes could form a backdrop for interchangeable subjects from other areas of the curriculum. Any lesson or topic that features music or songs could be displayed in this area.

Display

1. Study a song as part of another topic; in this example, Tudor music was the starting point in a history topic. The tune featured here was a folk song that was sung at executions by people as they watched a condemned person walk to their death – hence the title 'A Terrible Tudor Tune'.

2. Use a white backdrop for a stave, ensuring that the stave 'breaks' away from its normal structure towards the end of the board, as shown.

3. Place on it a series of notes from the song in the appropriate places.

4. Where the stave breaks up, start tilting and moving the notes from their correct position to give the impression that they are 'flying' away from the stave. (The notes could also increase in size, as if the music were too big to be contained by the stave.)

5. Position the lyrics of the song along the bottom of the stave.

6. Encourage children to add other work from the topic around the display.

7. This display can enhance the more permanent decoration in the room, which could be large versions of different notes around the walls.

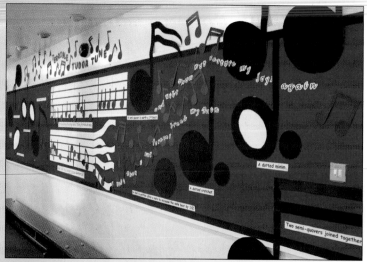

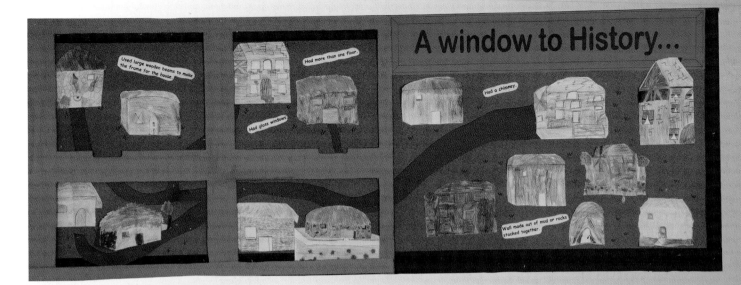

Cross-curricular Links

- **History:** organise a day related to the theme. For example, a Tudor day when the children dress up and experience the clothes that different people from society wore. Make a 'window to history' display. Behind the window create an image to represent the topic. Each panel of the window could be used to show a different aspect of the theme.

- **PE:** try out some dances related to the theme, for example, courtly dances from King Henry VIII's time.

- **Geography:** compare the chosen song with others from different countries. Examine the different ways in which the song could be sung and performed.

- **Music:** children could sing the song together and experiment with different musical instruments as accompaniment.

- **Literacy/Drama:** look at changing the song into a story or a play, filling in the 'before' and 'after' events. Extend this into small groups performing their plays.

- **Art:** using charcoal or chalk pastel, ask the children to try and represent the feelings they have from listening to the song. Limit them to simple patterns with no specific images.

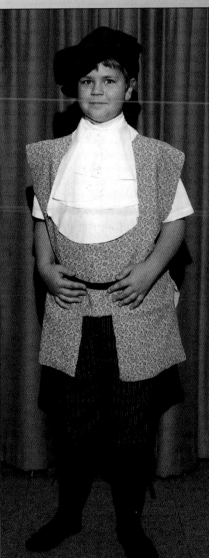

Shared Areas

Shared areas provide fantastic opportunities to display work and should aim to reflect the many activities that take place there. They are ideal spaces for showing some of the work achieved by small groups of children; it can help them define their area and take pride in their accomplishments. By displaying both class and group work in 'high traffic' areas a real class identity can be achieved and all children can feel involved in their environment. The intention of the shared area display shown here was to encourage children to start talking about and recognising their own strengths and identities.

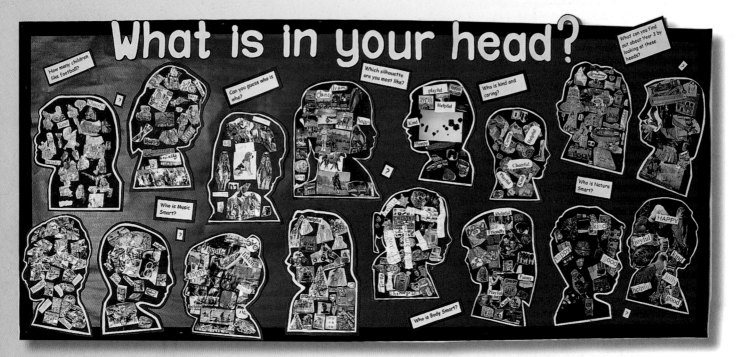

Display

1. Use a circle time session to discuss how we are all individual and have different ideas and thoughts, likes and dislikes. Discuss how we can be 'smart' in different ways, such as 'body smart' – an encompassing term associated with children who are good at sports or very active. The idea is that children can recognise they are smart at something without necessarily being academic. See page 30 for more information on SMART.

2. In pairs, let the children discuss these ideas further and make a list of all the things they like, their plans for the future, how they are 'smart', and their thoughts about what is going on in their life. All the things in their head!

3. Ask the children to cut out pictures from old catalogues and magazines to represent what is on their list.

4. Use an overhead projector to draw a silhouette of the children's heads on black sugar paper and cut them out.

5. Stick all their cuttings onto the black silhouette and add labels describing their personality.

6. Mount the heads on a brightly coloured background and add labels, such as: 'Who is body smart?', 'Who is music smart?' or 'Can you guess who is who?'. Finish the display with a title of 'What is in your head?'.

Cross-curricular Links

- **Art:** make papier-mâché heads, following the same idea, but these will be 3D. The children can make a collection of objects to represent what is in their head to put inside.

- **Art:** create 'funky frames'. The children decorate around the edges of their own frame with images and cut-outs of their favourite activities. Display and add labels asking questions such as, 'Can you guess the theme for each frame?'. They could put a self-portrait or photo in the frame.

- **History:** time capsule. Each child could create their own special time capsule to represent what is in their head now and their plans for when they are 18. They can then seal it and open it when they are 18 to see what they were thinking as a child compared to their ideas and ambitions as an adult.

- **Literacy:** look at characters in stories and think about what might be in their heads during the story. Children could act out scenes or pretend to be that character and answer questions from the class.

- **Speaking and listening:** children could play games, such as charades where they have to mime, or taboo where they have to describe 'What is in your head?' without using prohibited words, for example, they would have to try to describe a pencil without being able to say (or act) wood, lead, write, draw or sharpen.

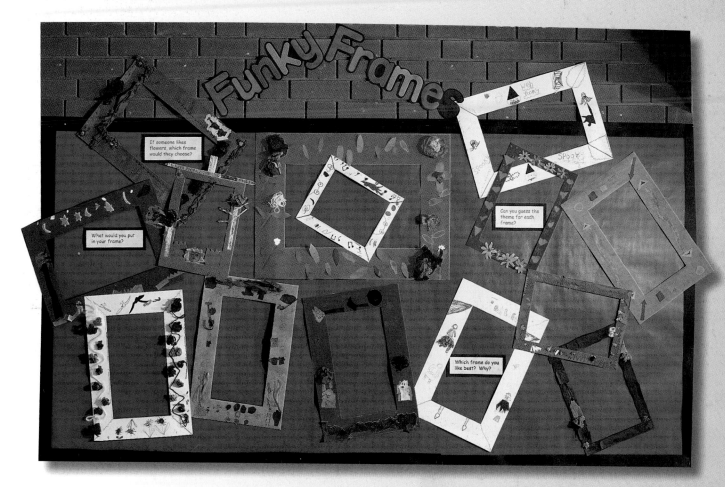

Reading Areas

Theme your reading areas to make them more exciting and inviting places for children to discover books. As with other communal spaces, the reading area can be linked to the whole school theme. Displays in this area are traditionally based on books that have formed part of a lesson. Where possible, centralise all the reading books so there is a focal point for reading in the school. The reading area can then be used for short sessions where children spend the time reading or choosing a new book. These areas should also have comfortable seating for the children to share a book with friends or an adult – the overall aim being that the environment becomes a relaxing place. In the example shown here, children have chosen their favourite books as a theme for the display.

Display

1. Create a background to give the impression of wooden panelling.

2. Give the children a selection of cereal packets and ask them to paint a representation of their favourite book.

3. Ensure they paint the spines as well as the front views to help make a varied display.

4. Ask the children to write a review on the back of their 'book'.

5. Make shelves out of hard plastic sheets, and attach them to the display board with string.

6. Display the books, some showing the spine, some facing outwards.

7. Locate the display in or near the reading area so that children can read the reviews and look at the artwork to help identify a book they might like to read.

8. To complete the display, ask the children to research their favourite author. Use charcoal to create author portraits and position these around the shelves. Label them and make a banner, 'Our Favourite Books'.

Allan Ahlberg

Jacqueline Wilson

Further Ideas

- Create a whole school reading room that features a central theme such as a jungle, the ocean or space. Display prominently key books that are linked to the theme. See page 6 for a jungle library idea.

- Identify a zone that deals with specific topics, where the children can go for research. Provide a table for children to write about a topic, and a listening station to make use of audio sources.

- Use a small tent, as shown, for a class based reading area. This helps to engage the children's desire to use the space. Inside the tent you can hang prompt cards to help challenge their thinking.

- Set up a buddy system whereby older children share books with the lower school. This session can be used to generate a mixed year group piece of work with the older children monitoring the younger ones' responses to a book and helping them to write reviews.

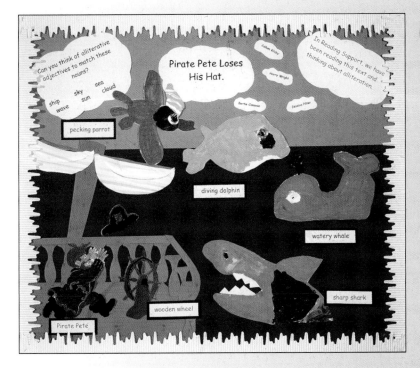

Cross-curricular Links

- **Literacy:** make a character profile from a story by drawing around the outline of a child and use collage materials to decorate it. Alternatively, fill the silhouette with key words from the text.

- **Literacy:** create a display based on a popular reading book, to show the main character and key words from the text. This display should be located in or near the reading area and can be used as a tool to help children read the text. In the example, (left), Pirate Pete (from the book by Kim Kennedy published by Harry N. Abrams, Inc.) was used to focus the children's attention on alliteration.

- **Drama:** the children could act out key scenes or dialogue from a class text.

Staff Room

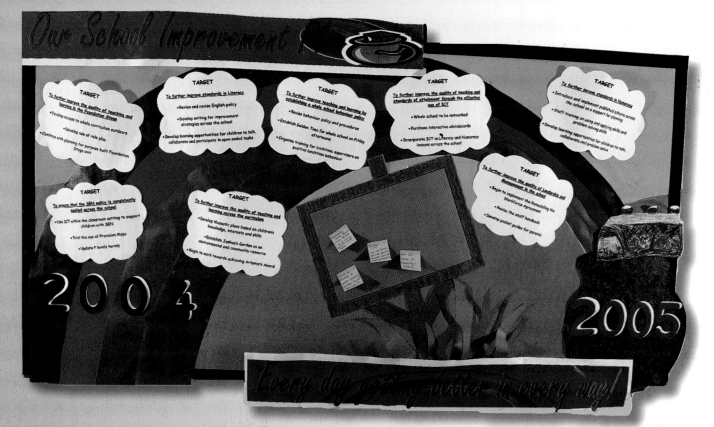

The staff room is often neglected but can play an important role in an interactive environment, with displays aimed at staff and visitors rather than examples of children's work. For example, the school improvement plan can be made into a display in an effort to involve and inform all the staff in the process and their understanding of it. By sharing and highlighting the completion of goals, staff can become motivated and this can follow through to their own development and training. The example here shows targets and ways of working towards them. It includes a space for staff to put up their own notices and swap ideas. The staff room can become an information station for staff and visitors alike, showing where the school is and where it is heading.

Display

1. Back half the board in blue and half in green to denote the earth and the sky and frame with a plain black border.

2. Cut curves into the green backing paper to form hills on the horizon.

3. Cut out coloured paper to make a rainbow, crossing from one side of the board to the other. To achieve a sense of perspective ensure the rainbow is wider on one side of the board and thinner on the other.

4. Using black sugar paper, cut out a cauldron shape to represent a pot of gold at the end of the rainbow.

5. Ask the children to create a picture of the school to be positioned on the pot at the end of the rainbow.

6. Label the start and finish with the current academic year dates, thereby creating a one-year time scale across the rainbow.

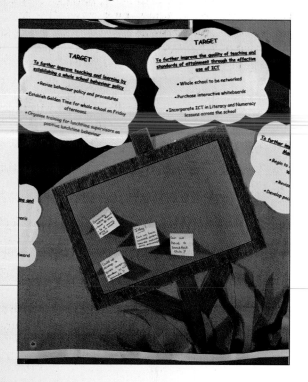

7. Type out the school improvement targets on white paper and cut into cloud shapes. Place these on and around the rainbow.

8. As each target is achieved, highlight the target and move the clouds along the rainbow.

9. Design a small notice board at the front of the rainbow so that staff can put up their own ideas and suggestions for further school improvements.

Further Ideas

● Further ideas for displaying a school improvement plan are frogs on a pond, leaves on a tree or boats crossing a lake, as shown here. Each boat is linked to one of the main targets in the school improvement plan, which are displayed on the 'Sailing Times' board. At either end of the lake are two signs, showing the start and end of the year. As the school makes progress on each school improvement target, the corresponding boat sails across the lake towards the year end. Once the target is achieved the boat is moored at the far side of the lake.

● Revamp the career and professional development board to stimulate staff and inform them of possibilities available to them.

● A social events board can be created to highlight forthcoming staff outings and to put forward ideas or plan new events. This can be effective in creating a fun atmosphere and building good relationships amongst staff.

● A 'curriculum board' could show important dates and events across the year groups; it could suggest what resources are available or need to be ordered.

Numeracy Displays

Numeracy is one of the highest frequency lessons, so it is important to have a prominent and usable numeracy display in every classroom. The display can be made interactive by including the children's own questions and numeracy puzzles. In this example, the focus was money and problem solving.

Display

1. Create templates of bank notes in different colours and denominations, and distribute them to the class, ensuring that children in the same ability group are given the same colour.

2. Ask each child to write a word problem involving money on their bank note. You should aim for a different level of difficulty of word problem for each bank note colour.

3. Display the notes so that they can be used by the class as a challenge when they have finished their work.

4. Widen the display by including coins as well.

5. Pose some generic questions or challenges on the display, in addition to the individual problems written on each note. For example, 'How many different ways are there of making £100?' or ' What is the highest amount you can make using just two purple notes and one green?'.

20

- **Numeracy:** create a giant calculator that uses a hundred square as its keypad. Stick a large number of multi-coloured numbers coming out from the calculator, up the wall and even onto the ceiling. Use these numbers to pose questions for the class to answer, such as: 'What is the total of all the yellow numbers?' or 'What is the highest amount that can be made using just a pink and a blue number?'. Ask children to devise their own questions so that the display can be changed regularly. Ensure that the questions can be easily removed from the display and show the solutions on the back so that the children can quickly check their answers.

- **Numeracy:** use a 'Mathamagician'. Find a fancy dress hat and cape that children can put on when they are not feeling confident on a given question. Create a simple chant that the class say to help the child. Alternatively, you could have a session where the children challenge the teacher to answer questions posed by the rest of the class. The hat and cape can be worn by the challenger.

- **Numeracy:** draw the image of a wizard onto coloured paper and cut it out. Attach it to a different coloured background. Cut out pumpkins from orange paper and cauldrons from black paper to position at random around the wizard. Display numeracy work on each pumpkin and cauldron. The work can be changed to correspond to the topics being taught. Title the display 'We are Number Smart' (see page 14 and page 30 for more information on SMART).

- **Art:** when studying shape and space, ask the class to see if they can identify any shapes in modern abstract art. Carry this through into an art lesson when children are asked to create pictures solely using shape templates in a particular artistic style.

- **PSHCE:** use the numeracy display as an aspect for celebration in the class, by encouraging children to have a go at the questions asked and devising their own; or celebrating another step on the class target board.

Literacy Displays

A display can be much more than just a showcase for the children's work. A large display can become a backdrop or visual representation of a scene from a class study text. This can become a great focal point for the ensuing lessons, for drama sessions or for character hot seating. A large display such as this can become a class project, involving all the children in its creation. This gives them greater ownership of their classroom and demonstrates a really creative way in which to access a text.

Display

1. Select a scene with strong imagery from the text that the class is studying; this example features the witches from Macbeth that have been painted by the children.

2. Hang a dark green background on which to create the tree. Use scrunched up, twisted pieces of paper for the roots, bark and branches. These can be glued or stapled to the background.

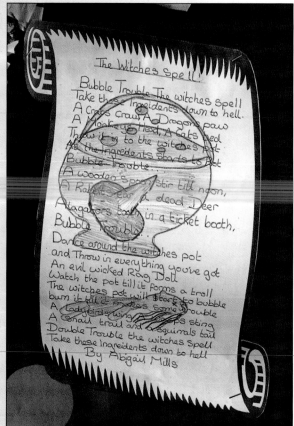

3. Build up the paper into the shape of a tree, which can be painted to look more realistic or covered with images and extracts from, or connected to, the text, such as pictures or a biography of the author, or the location of the scene. In this example, however, it has been left undecorated, which is still striking.

4. Add extra decoration produced by the class that relates to the text, for example, a cauldron and bats.

5. Work from follow-up sessions can then be displayed. Here, the class was asked to create their own spells, written on a scroll template.

Cross-curricular Links

- **Literacy:** create a display that focuses on structuring the children's writing. Here, a 'Writing Rocket' is used to show the children various steps in their writing to achieve 'lift off'. Each label in the countdown shows a different stage in composing a sentence. The children can refer to it to check their work. The countdown labels can be changed to reflect the topic being taught, for example, the five stages to recounting a text. This display has also incorporated elements of self-evaluation and styles of writing.

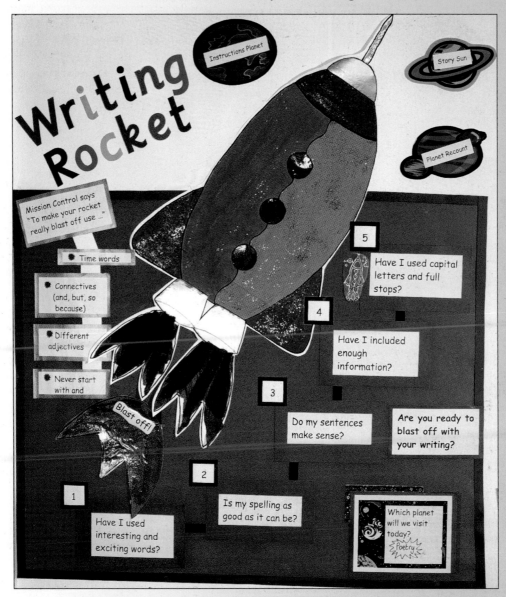

- **Drama:** use the display as a backdrop for drama sessions, based on scenes from the text. Alternatively, the children can use or refer to the display when impersonating a character during hot seating.

- **PSHCE:** translate an idea from the text, in this example, spell-making, into a circle time session. Ask the group to suggest, individually or collectively, a spell about their hopes and fears for the future.

- **Design and Technology:** get the children to design, make and advertise items related to the text, in this example, potions or drinks.

- **Art:** continue the skills involved in making the display in their art lessons. The children could make models or additional props for the scene on display or suggested in the text.

- **Geography:** use the display to help focus the children's research into the environment in which the text is set.

Interactive Displays

Displaying finished work or large images is a great way to promote a welcoming environment in the classroom. However, it is not necessary for every display to be about generated work or the topic the class is studying. It can be beneficial to use display space as a teaching aid. Why not use the space to provide key grammar and sentence building words relevant to the age of the class? Just as we would create a writing frame or list appropriate language at the start of our lessons, why not have a permanent space that the class can refer to? The words on display can be changed as the class progresses. In this example, key words can be removed to build sentences.

Display

1. Back a display in a medium to dark colour.

2. Draw an outline of a sweet jar on card and cut out. Use this as a template to produce more sweet jars.

3. Use coloured paper to make some simple weighing scales.

4. Word process all the relevant key words and capital letters and photocopy them onto brightly coloured paper.

5. Cut out each word in the shape of a sweet and individual capital letters in the shape of a lollipop.

6. Stick the words onto the jars, as shown.

7. Cut long thin strips of brown sugar paper and mount them onto the board to form a shelf. Using a black or brown marker draw a wood grain effect on the shelf.

8. Mount the jars onto the shelf.

9. Word process a title banner for the display as well as questions asking the children to sort the key words into different categories.

Further Ideas

- **Literacy:** make a display based on a simple story. In this example, the school has used the Teddy Bears' Picnic. Children were asked to make 'adjective sandwiches', which are displayed on the picnic cloth. The children also painted their own teddy bears to decorate the board. The class can refer to this board when they need to think of an adjective.

- **PSHCE:** use a similar device to help children empathise with different characters in stories. Ask the children to create cards, each showing a different emotion, so that each child has a bank of emotion cards. The children can then be asked to choose what they feel is an appropriate emotion for any given situation in the texts that they study.

- **Art/Literacy:** the children work in groups to make 'silly noun cereals'. Empty cereal packets can be covered in white paper and painted to make the new 'products'. Children can choose any noun they like and add it to a cereal variety, such as flakes, snaps, or crispies. They can then design their cereal box and describe the look and taste, for example, 'Planet Pops – green gooey planets covered in chocolate – they taste out of this world!'. The finished cereal boxes could be displayed on a shelf as in a supermarket (see Reading Areas

display instructions for a shelf, page 16). To finish the display, price labels could be made to go beneath each product.

- **Literacy:** create a punctuation paddling pool. Fill a paddling pool with objects that you would normally find when paddling. On the front of these objects attach different types of punctuation (you will need several of each type) and on the back put a definition of what they mean and how they are used. The children can then fetch a specific punctuation object to put on their desk as they work. Alternatively, as a class you could send a child to go 'fishing' for the correct punctuation. You can then check with the class to see if the right one has been 'caught' and ask them to explain how that punctuation is used.

PSHCE Displays

Creating a PSHCE or circle time display in the classroom can give a strong focal point for current and future class discussions. Such displays can be interactive and allow the children to consider their own thoughts, feelings and beliefs, which they can share with others. This can be particularly useful when encouraging speaking and listening skills by asking children to discuss their feelings about their work or to give a short presentation about themselves to the class.

Display

1. Instigate a discussion in class about different emotions and record them on the board.

2. Ask a couple of children to come to the front of the class and mime or act out a range of emotions. The rest of the class has to try and guess the correct emotion.

3. Ask the children to select one emotion and then to draw a representation of it. Restrict them by allowing no specific images and limit them to just repeating lines or patterns. Provide chalk pastels to colour their designs, but only allow each child a limited palette.

4. Mount the finished artworks on black paper, grouping similar emotions together.

5. Display with large images depicting the emotions that link to other topics, such as weather, as shown above.

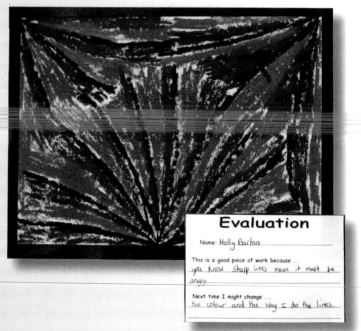

- **PSHCE:** create an 'All about me' board. This can be a permanent display that individual children can contribute to on a weekly basis. The board would allow the children to discuss themselves in a context outside lessons, as well as celebrating their extra-curricular achievements. The board could feature prompts to help the children, such as: 'Where I live' and 'My friends are ...'. The children should be encouraged to bring in pictures and objects from home and to take ownership of the display. The week's chosen child could then present the display to the class, talking about the various aspects of their life that they want to share.

- **PSHCE:** using their bank of emotion cards (see page 25), allow the children to put up an emotion that reflects how they are feeling each morning. This can lead to discussion based on their choices.

- **PSHCE/Geography:** examine how we feel in relation to other things, such as the weather. For example, how do the children feel when it is raining? When it is windy? In PSHCE or circle time sessions the same technique can be used to encourage children to listen and verbalise their feelings. Using white boards, the children could draw their feelings based on situations presented in the session.

- **Literacy/History:** the above method can also be used to help the children empathise with characters and situations in texts or periods that they are studying.

- **Science:** the children could design an investigation into the colours we associate with emotions. Is it accurate to link red with anger? Is this true of the whole class?

- **Geography:** extend the study into the wider world and examine how colour is used to convey meaning. Look at road and warning signs and magazine advertisements.

Celebration Displays

Display should celebrate the children's work, as well as inform. Celebration can take many forms, a piece of artwork, a certificate or an award, or even an assembly. All of these should be shown off to their best advantage and it is possible to do this through one single display. The firework display shown here enables three different celebrations to be displayed at once, the Fizz, Whizz and Bang Awards. In this school the year group has three classes. Every two weeks, two children from each class have a piece of work chosen to be celebrated. The work is displayed on the award board and parents are invited to view their children's work.

Starting Points

1. Back a large display board with a navy blue or other dark coloured paper.

2. Draw out six rocket fireworks in different colours, two for each award – Fizz, Whizz and Bang. You may wish to make more or less depending on the size of your display. The main burst of the firework should be large enough to act as a mount for an A4 piece of paper.

3. Staple the fireworks onto your board, pointing in different directions.

4. Use either the computer or cut-out letters to create a title for the display. Ideas for titles are: 'Firework Celebrations'; '5 4 3 2 1 CELEBRATE!' or 'Rocket Celebrations'.

5. On the tail of each rocket attach a title to show what it is celebrating, for example, Handwriting or Swimming. Then add the child's name for the piece of work being celebrated.

Further Ideas

- Use characters to represent different achievements. In this example, child-friendly characters called Splats have been created to support different aspects of good behaviour. Supersplat is the term used to refer to children chosen each week for following the school's golden rules well (see page 38).

- Recognising positive behaviour can also be demonstrated through more individual and visual methods, such as placing a gold star on the back of children's chairs so that anyone visiting will know of their achievements. The display below shows other ways that good behaviour can be highlighted.

- A cabinet could be used in the classroom to display 3D work, trophies and medals linked to work exhibited on the main board.

Cross-curricular Links

- **Literacy:** look at traditional stories and at any celebrations that take place in the story. For example, what does Cinderella have to celebrate at the start of the fairy tale? Compare and contrast this to what she has to celebrate at the end of the story.

- **Design and Technology:** design a certificate that could be awarded to all the children whose work is displayed on the celebration board.

- **Art:** design and make cards for various celebrations throughout the year to display on the board. As the board is intended to be updated regularly you may want each child to design their name exploding out of a firework as a reusable label to identify their work on display.

- **ICT:** A screen saver on the class computer or an interactive white board can show more pictures of work or certificates when not in use.

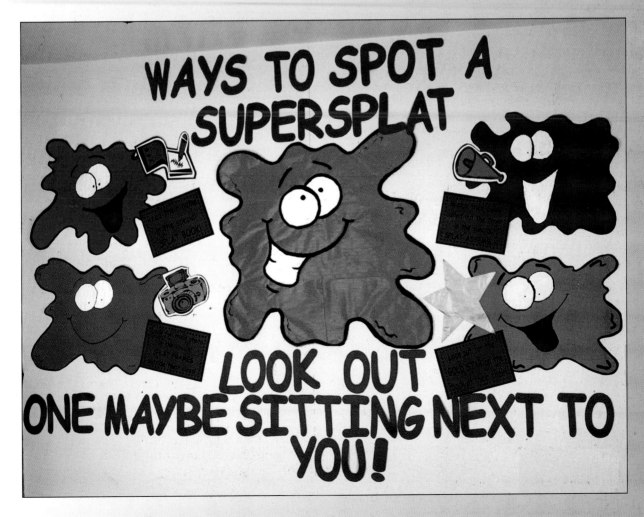

How Are You SMART?

Children excel in different ways and the school environment should encourage and celebrate their individual strengths. This can be achieved through their school work, or by children presenting to the class about their outside interests. An interactive learning environment should heighten the children's awareness of their own strengths and help them feel more confident in their learning. SMART is a term used to describe something the child is smart at doing. Here are some examples you could consider:

Number Smart: those who enjoy working with numbers and are good at working out sums.
Word Smart: those who like writing letters and stories and are good at spelling.
Self Smart: those who know their feelings and set themselves targets.
Body Smart: those who are good at sport and are very active.
2D/3D Smart: those who are good at making models, drawing and painting.
Music Smart: those who enjoy singing and are good at playing a musical instrument.
People Smart: those who enjoy the company of others and are able to socialise and communicate well with people of all ages.

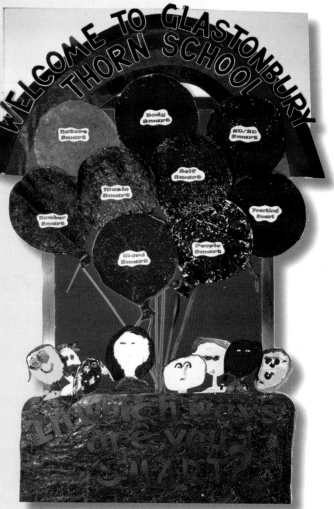

Display

1. Back a large board with a sky blue colour. Cut out large balloon shapes from white card to provide one for each SMART area.

2. Cover each balloon with a different texture. In this example the children used foodstuffs, such as pasta, cereal, nuts, dried beans and rice, which were stuck on and then painted in bright colours.

3. Label each balloon to represent a different SMART area.

4. Cut out a basket shape from a large piece of card; a wicker effect can be achieved by gluing on bran cereal and painting it brown.

5. Mount the balloons on the top half of the board, bunched together and leave a space before mounting the 'basket'.

6. Join the balloons to the basket using strips of coloured paper.

7. Let the children paint self-portraits and display them in the basket to reinforce the message that we are all SMART at something.

Cross-curricular Links

- **PSHCE:** display children's self-portraits on a yellow sun background to create a 'sunshine strengths' board. Ask the children to write down on strips of yellow card what they feel are their own strengths. Attach these as rays of light, radiating out from the sun portraits, to give a nice, bright image.

- **PSHCE:** set up a house or team system in the class (or whole school) and ask the children to examine the different strengths that each can bring to their house or team. Use their ideas to create a motto to represent each house or team.

- **Design and Technology/PSHCE:** make an animal, incorporating levers and split pins to allow moving parts, here crocodiles were made to reflect the class identity. Display them on a background of yellow paper to represent sand, with a blue paper river running across it. During a circle time session, discuss ways in which we can care for each other and write them in individual hearts. Position a heart over each animal.

- **PSHCE:** create an 'All about me' board, to give the children the opportunity to talk about themselves and their achievements (see also page 27).

- **Literacy:** use self-evaluation to help the children become more aware of their strengths in their written work. Ask them to underline three things they most like in their own or a friend's work and then to explain why.

Learning Styles

It has become increasingly important to understand how we learn as well as how we teach. We all learn in different ways. Some of us learn well by using visual resources (visual learners), others prefer to learn through listening (auditory learners) and there are those who learn by using practical methods (kinaesthetic learners). In our classrooms all three learning styles are equally important. It is therefore essential to share this understanding with the children, parents and visitors.

The Learning Styles game pictured below enables the player to find out which style of learning they enjoy best. The children answer questions by placing a blue disc onto one of three learning style mats. At the end of the questions the mat with the most discs shows their preferred learning style. You may wish to label the learning style mats with more child-friendly vocabulary (auditory – hear-ers, kinaesthetic – do-ers and visual – see-ers). Younger children would understand that they learn best by seeing, doing or hearing things as the posters shown above demonstrate.

Making the Game

1. Using A3 coloured paper, make three learning style mats. Each mat should be labelled with the learning style and have a picture or symbol as a visual representation. For example, at the top of the auditory mat, it could say: 'We learn best by using our ears'. In the middle would be a large picture or symbol of an ear and then in large letters across the bottom 'Hear-ers' or 'Auditory learners', depending on the age of the children.

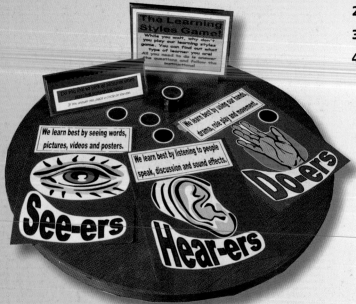

2. Laminate all three mats.

3. Cut out blue discs from card, or supply counters.

4. Devise nine questions, three for each learning style, and type them onto strips of card. After each question write instructions on where to place the disc. Here are some examples:

   – (Auditory learners): Do you learn best when you are listening to your teacher talking about something new? If the answer is yes place a blue disc on the Hear-ers mat.

   – (Kinaesthetic learners): Do you learn best when you are making something? If the answer is yes place a blue disc on the Do-ers mat.

   – (Visual learners): Do you learn best when you are watching a TV programme about something new? If the answer is yes place a blue disc on the See-ers mat.

Further Ideas

In order for the children to think about how they are learning and to develop their understanding of learning they need to be frequently reminded. This can be achieved through the following activities.

- Class chant: devise a class chant that can be repeated at the start of every lesson so the children recognise that they are about to learn something new. An example of a chant you may wish to use is: teacher, 'Are you ready to learn?'; children, 'Show me, tell me, and let me do!'. This can be reinforced with hand actions, such as fingers from the eyes out for 'show me'; fingers from the ears out for 'tell me' and waving hands in the air for 'let me do!'.

- Learning style posters (see page 32) can be used to explain each learning style and what it means. They should be large, bright, colourful and clearly displayed in a prominent position in the classroom for all to see, and regularly referred to.

- Encourage children to understand fully the way in which they learn by asking one group to suggest an activity to help another group learn. For example, you could ask the visual learners to create an activity for the auditory learners.

- Science: explore the left and right sides of the brain and the different functions attached to each half. Let the children work in small groups to create a large brain. Make cards to represent the different functions of the right and left side of the brain and ask the children to position them correctly.

- Science: look at what our brains and minds need. Ask the children to discuss what we need to keep our brains healthy: water, food, happiness and so on. Glue a colourful brain to a backing sheet and stick paper hearts all around it. In each heart place a child's drawing of the important things our brain needs.

Mind Mapping

Asking the children to write down everything they know about a subject is a good way to introduce new topics and start discussions. This idea can be taken further and developed into a simple framework that can eventually be applied to any subject. The 'I know, I think, I wonder' board, shown here, provides a clear apparatus to display the children's ideas and questions.

The children start by writing down anything they may already know about a subject, followed by what they 'think' – things that they are not sure about. Finally, the children are invited to ask ('wonder') what they would like to know about the new topic. By incorporating the answers to their questions into your planning, you are enabling the children to take a more active role in what they learn, and the environment in which they are learning becomes interactive.

Display

1. Take a dark but colourful backdrop.

2. Using an overhead projector, enlarge the image of a child and trace the image onto white paper.

3. Allow the children to paint in the details of the image.

4. Mount the image onto the board, leaving space to put three clouds around it, each cloud bearing one of the labels: I know, I think or I wonder.

5. Make a banner with a heading: 'I know, I think, I wonder'. Add a large label showing the current topic; in this example it is 'Sunny Days and Holidays'.

6. Using small labels, ask the children to write down their ideas and questions about the topic.

7. Display the labels and share them with the rest of the class.

8. Look at the questions they have asked and try to incorporate the answers into your planning.

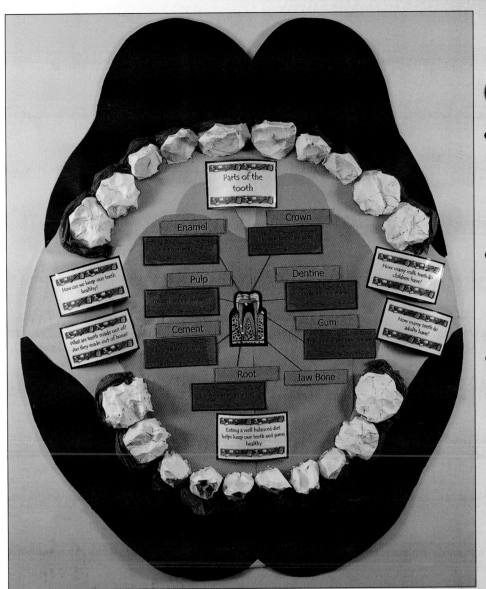

Further Ideas

- Art: ask the children to design a logo for each new topic to be displayed on the board as a visual reminder of what they are studying, for example, a sun logo for 'Sunny Days and Holidays'.

- Referring to the 'I know, I think, I wonder' display, the children can record the whole class's responses in their books as a starting point or title page to the new topic.

- Speaking and listening: use the questions on the display to encourage 'talking partners'. Ask the children to discuss their ideas. Can they clear up one another's misconceptions? This can be developed more with older children. The questions could be asked at the start of every lesson, for each topic.

- Set up a display for a specific topic. Initially, show the children's questions about the topic and over the course of the session replace the questions with the children's work as those questions become answered. In the example above, the topic is teeth and the children have worked together to create a 3D mouth with labels and questions about parts of the tooth.

- Self-evaluation: create a similar display, entitled 'Think about it' (see right) that focuses on the plenary at the end of a lesson. Post questions so the children think about what they have learned: 'What did you find difficult learning about...?'; 'What helped you the most while working on ...?'; 'Is there anything that could help you more about ...?'; 'What do we now know from this lesson?'; 'What do we still want to know?'.

Self-evaluation

Encouraging the children to use self-evaluation is essential for the development of their knowledge and understanding. It can be quite difficult for children to verbalise their thoughts and feelings about their own work, especially the younger ones. Here, a simple framework of easy, everyday concepts helps the children to evaluate their own work. The 'Hit, Miss or Maybe' board asks the children to compare what they have achieved against the lesson's learning intention. The children have to give a 'thumbs up', 'thumbs down' or 'thumbs in the middle' response to how difficult they found the task and then evaluate their work with one of the three options. As their confidence grows the children can begin to explain what it is they have done and how they decided on their rating. In this example the children evaluated abstract images they created in Art.

Display

1. Back the board in a strong colour so that the work stands out.

2. Cut a large template with jagged edges, big enough to frame an A4 piece of work, to serve as a permanent background on which the children's work is directly mounted.

3. Ensure that each child in the class has a mounting and display their name underneath it.

4. Create a class set of coloured thumbs, about the same size as a hand, in the three positions: thumb up (green), thumb down (red) and thumb in the middle (orange), so that they tie in with the traffic light system.

5. Laminate the thumbs so that they can be written on and wiped clean.

6. Make a title banner for the board, 'Hit, Miss or Maybe – Our Self-Evaluation Board'. Add three explanatory labels for the 'Hit, Miss and Maybe thumbs'. Here they refer to WALT, which stands for 'We are learning to …' that is used to introduce the learning objective at the start of each lesson.

7. Display children's work on a weekly basis. Each week, ask the children to choose an appropriate thumb for their work and then to write on the thumbs an explanation for their choice for that piece of work. Position the thumbs alongside the work.

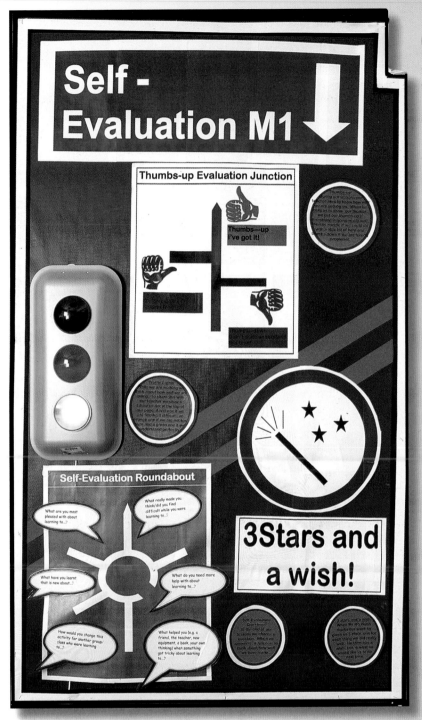

Further Ideas

- Traffic light system: this works in a similar way to the self-evaluation board, with the children using the colours red, orange and green to denote their understanding of a concept (red for 'I do not understand' through to green for understanding). It can be used to show a child's progress through a lesson with the children being asked at regular intervals to draw an appropriate coloured circle in the margin of their books thereby recording their understanding.

- Wow books: a Wow book is an individual scrapbook for each child. The book contains examples of their best work, or work from the 'Hit, Miss and Maybe' board that they have evaluated themselves. The book can become a useful record of their progress as well as a portfolio of their work.

- Peer evaluation: group the children into pairs and ask them to evaluate each other's work and then explain their reasoning to their partner. This is also a great way to encourage their speaking and listening skills. As the children progress through school this can be developed. The children can fill out a more formal self-evaluation ticket that can be placed on any display. Eventually they can be asked to evaluate every piece of work in their books, or with their partners using self-marking or highlighting the three best aspects and areas needing improvement in their work.

- Artwork appreciation: artwork is difficult to assess, therefore this is an excellent way for the children to learn to appreciate their art and make positive criticisms of their own and other's work.

- The various ways in which the children evaluate their work can be summed up in a display such as the one above, where familiar road signs are used as a way of showing a range of self-evaluation methods. Three stars and a wish is a style of marking used in the classroom. When marking work, the teacher gives a star to three things the child has done well. At the end of the work there may be a wish that the teacher would like to see in the next piece. The wish is equivalent to a target and is represented by drawing a wand.

Golden Time

Golden time is a positive behaviour strategy that rewards all children. Operated within a classroom the children have the opportunity to spend 30 minutes at the end of the week, enjoying an activity not normally provided by the curriculum. The time can be reduced in increments of five minutes depending on the behaviour of the children during the week. There are golden rules that the children have to follow to keep their golden time.

The golden time scheme can be operated on a whole school basis, encouraging interaction across the age groups through play. Decide what activities will be available and ask the children to choose an activity that will last for the duration of a half term. Children who have lost part of their golden time have to congregate in one central area and are encouraged to think about their actions. To remind the children of how they behave and what they have chosen as their golden time activity, a golden time display can be used.

Display

1. Cut out large leaf templates for two palm trees from green backing paper.

2. Write the golden rules on brightly coloured card, cut them out and stick one rule onto each leaf.

3. For the tree trunks, cut a series of wedge-shaped squares from brown paper. These squares should gradually decrease in size from bottom to top.

4. Mount the leaves at the top of the trunks.

5. Choose a large space to display the golden time trees. Framing an opening or window works well, or position them at the front of the hall to ensure their message is clearly visible to all.

Golden Rules

Do be gentle	Do not hurt anybody
Do be kind and helpful	Do not hurt people's feelings
Do work hard	Do not waste your or other people's time
Do look after property	Do not waste or damage things
Do listen to people	Do not interrupt
Do be honest	Do not cover up the truth

Further Ideas

- Make a small display board for the classroom that repeats the golden rules for the class. This board can also be used to keep track of how much golden time each child has. In the above example, children's names on stars are moved down the rainbow if they lose any time. Make warning cards to give to children who are running out of golden time.

- Another idea is to create a board (see left) that explains how golden time works and what happens if a child breaks a golden rule. Linking this to Splats (see page 29) can help to reinforce good behaviour.

- Children who earn their full golden time each week over a long period could be rewarded. One way is to have a sweet shop display with lots of different cardboard chocolate bars. If a child manages to achieve full golden time for several weeks they could be rewarded by choosing a 'chocolate bar' from the display. On the back of each bar write a reward, such as a prize of a small sweet or an extra ten minutes on their next golden time session.

- A supplementary display could depict the different types of activities the children could choose for their golden time. This could also be used to help keep track of their choices. You could also leave a space for the children to post their own suggestions for what they would like to do in golden time.

Reward Activities

The idea of having specific options for golden time can be extended to last for the duration of a half term. The children choose their option, for example, Football, Chess, French or Music and stick to it for the time allocated. This method allows more time for the teacher or teaching assistant to plan and organise the activities. Having set activities gives a sense of structure to the golden time sessions, which can help the children to control their behaviour. These options can be turned into a large golden time display, which can increase awareness of golden time as well as remind the children of their chosen activities. Located in a large, communal space the display can act as a visual aid for the children to maintain their behaviour until golden time at the end of the week.

Display

1. Draw a large treasure chest, with the lid open, to place at the bottom of the display.

2. Decide which activities will be offered for the next half term, or whatever period of time that you decide.

3. Create large images to represent each activity. To do this cut a simple template out of card in the required shape, for example, a paintbrush and palette to represent Art. Use screwed up tissue paper, glued onto the template, to add colour and texture.

4. Position the images as if they were flying out of the box – this is an ideal opportunity to break out of borders or cover a large expanse of bare wall.

5. As a reminder, you could add to each image the names of all the children who have chosen that activity.

6. Ensure this is displayed in a communal area so that all the children can be reminded of their choices and of the desired behaviour.

Golden Time

🦆 **Be gentle**
Be kind 🦆
🦆 **Be honest**
Do listen 🦆
🦆 **Take care**
Work hard 🦆

Further Ideas

- It is possible to link golden time with other behavioural strategies, for example, arranging the children into school 'houses'. Rather than just applying the house system to major events, such as sports day, the loss of golden time could have an impact upon that child's house points, so that the idea of supporting a house becomes linked with behaviour. To reinforce the children's awareness of this, banners could be made to depict each house, showing the golden rules and hung in a prominent shared space, such as the hall.

- At the start of golden time you could bring the whole school together to sing a communal song that signifies the start of the session.

- A golden time assembly can be used to celebrate a selection of children from each class who have followed the golden rules.

- Children, who follow the golden rules well, could be appointed as Golden Monitors, responsible for getting out and putting away all the golden time equipment.

- Other children could be Golden Spotters, who look out for good behaviour during break and lunch times. A few minutes could be allotted to them in the golden time assembly to report their findings. (They could even wear a uniform – a cap, badge or sash – to add prestige to their role.)

- 'Golden Oscars': at the end of the year you may want to hold the 'Golden Oscars' as a celebration for all the children who have never lost any golden time through the year. This can be as low key as an assembly or elaborated upon to include parents and the hire of a tux for the host teacher!

- To help children who often find it difficult to keep their golden time to understand the rules more clearly, involve them in the creation of their own display, as shown, (right). Challenge each child to draw an image to show how they think one particular golden rule could be kept. Display their drawings alongside the relevant rules where they can be clearly seen.

Behaviour Displays

There are many different ways in which behaviour can be managed. Apart from providing a constant, visual reminder of appropriate behaviour in the classroom, a display for behaviour can be interactive and even generated by the children. The idea of a board game is simple to implement. The children can be divided into teams and play for a small prize, or simply to win. Most importantly, the teams should be allowed to move their counters after demonstrating appropriate behaviour, so that the display becomes a positive aspect of the classroom. In this example, a giant space game was produced to cover part of the classroom ceiling.

Making the game

1. Using the space available create a simple track, divided into equal spaces, to form the basic structure on which the children will progress.

2. Agree upon the theme of your game, in this example a 'great space race' theme has been chosen. Ask the children to design appropriate images to decorate the track, so that they feel they are creating the game. Here, children have added planets, space ships, space stations, black holes and stars.

3. As a class, decide what kind of instructions can be placed on various squares to make the game more interesting, for example, 'You are under alien attack, roll a six to escape or miss a go'; 'You need to refuel, miss a go' or 'You are being sucked into a black hole, roll again to escape'.

4. Write 'chance' or 'forfeit' cards. These can be simple: 'Go back to start' or 'Miss a go' or more complex, such as: 'You have added a new hyper-drive to your ship, add two to your next three rolls of the dice'.

5. Create a different token (in this case space ships) for each team to act as their counter.

6. Make team sheets for the children to keep on their desks. It is a good idea to laminate these sheets for longer life, as the children need to write their names on them, but they have to be easily changeable should anyone be moved to a different table.

7. Provide a space on the board to list the teams. Award children a point to mark on their team sheets whenever they are behaving in an appropriate manner. Once a team reaches a tally of five, allow them to roll a dice and move their counter the corresponding amount on the board.

COST Of CAR PARTS

- ① = Ready to Start
  = lesson first ×5

- ② = Tidiest table at end of day ×3

- = completing work independently × 5

- = Kind and helpful to others × 5

  DRIVES SLOW

- = Kind and helpful to others × 10

  DRIVES FAST

Cross-curricular Links

Many different themes can be used as a basis for a behavioural game display. Here are a few ideas:

- **History:** the game can be linked to history topics – teams could be Victorian explorers sailing the Atlantic to claim territory in the name of Britain, or Viking invaders trying to conquer Britain.

- **Art:** use the lesson to create the additional images that decorate the display. Using chalk pastels and showing children how to blend colours together is a good way of keeping a structure and teaching a skill, while allowing them the freedom to choose the image.

- **Geography:** base the game on geographical landmarks, their local environment or different countries.

- **Numeracy:** car race. Each group of children has to earn the elements needed to build their car as shown in a car parts list, and then race them along a track. In the above example, to build a car with standard wheels and a slow driver they would have to earn three 'behaviour' points by having a tidy table for the wheels and five points for being kind and helpful for the driver. For better wheels and a faster driver they would have to earn five and ten points respectively. Points can be recorded on the parts sheet or on the white board. Children can decide to build a slower car and get moving along the board quickly or take the risk of waiting for enough points to build a faster car, which can then move along the board at a faster pace. Once the cars are 'built' they can start moving along the race track (top). A slow car has to earn five points to move one space, whereas a fast one only has to earn three marks to move the car one space.

5. **PSHCE:** create a board game based on friends, friendship and behaviour. Ask the children to design a convincing game based on their own experiences. Discuss what sort of dilemmas could be involved.

Incentive Displays

An interactive classroom offers possibilities for several behaviour incentives that can range from full displays to smaller pictures to remind children of appropriate behaviour, such as the sit, look, listen and think cards shown below. Make visual representations of these actions and display them in a prominent position in the classroom. They provide a non-verbal reminder for children to stay focused. You can simply point to a card or write a child's name underneath it, to indicate to a child what they should be doing.

The 'Tremendous Tree' display, (left) works on an individual level and can be used almost anywhere in the classroom – not necessarily on a board but on any spare wall space. The display features a bare tree; each time a child behaves in an appropriate manner they are rewarded with a leaf. They write their name on the leaf and stick it on the tree. At the end of a term or half term, all the leaves are taken down and put into a pot for one name to be pulled out to win a prize. The more leaves a child has the greater their chance of winning. This display works well if you do not always teach the same class as any child can be rewarded with a leaf, including those from different age groups.

Display

1. Back a board with green paper. You may prefer to split the backing between green and blue to suggest the ground and sky.

2. Draw a bare tree on brown paper, cut it out and place it on the board.

3. Use a black marker pen to add lines and details to make the tree seem more realistic.

4. Photocopy leaf templates onto green or autumnal coloured paper and pin them to a corner of the board so children can cut out and put up their own leaves.

Further Ideas

- Territory Tracks: this is aimed at younger children, based on the whole school jungle theme. Here, the class animal symbol, a crocodile, was used to create a winding path of animal footprints. The footprints lead to a specified destination or finish line. In this example, the tracks lead to a party, stopping along the way to pick up balloons, party clothes, and so forth. The children are divided into groups and each group marks off their progress on the tracks using coloured squares, which they receive for displaying desired behaviour. When each group reaches the end they are rewarded with a small 'party' or treat.

- Hot Spots: a hot spot is an approximately A4 sized red circle with the words hot spot written on it and pictures of flames. The hot spot is used to help children remain seated. Should a child earn a hot spot they are then responsible for keeping it hot by sitting on it. If the hot spot is not hot when you check it, or the child is out of their seat leaving the hot spot to get cold, they can earn a minor consequence, such as a minute off their break. Using the hot spot turns the problem into a game, which helps keep the children interested and more aware of their actions. When not in use the hot spots can be displayed on the wall or the board for people to see as a visual reminder. The hot spots become part of the environment, and the class can take pleasure in explaining their use to any visitors.

School Aims

It is important that schools have strong communication links both within and outside the school environment. In this area display is often overlooked. Display can be a bright, visual and highly effective way of communicating key messages, rather than having them written in a file or diary and forgotten. Such messages as the school's aims, slogan, mission statement and mottos can be placed in communal spaces as a constant reminder to staff and visitors alike. Here, the school has chosen to display their main aims in reception for all visitors to see.

Display

1. Take two long strips of cane and smaller lengths for rungs. Tie them together with string to make a ladder, ensuring the space between each rung is sufficient to fit an A4 sheet of laminated paper.

2. Repeat this process until you have enough ladders to display all your key messages.

3. Make sure you have enough rungs to fit one word of your main message per space.

4. Write or type out your school aims and slogans on brightly coloured A4 paper and laminate.

5. Attach the laminates to the ladders by either stapling them directly onto the canes or by using a hole punch and tying them to the rungs.

6. Draw around two children, lying in a climbing position, onto cardboard.

7. Cut them out and ask the children to finish them by pasting small squares of coloured paper, to represent the school uniform.

8. Attach the figures to either side of a ladder to give the impression that they are climbing, indicating that the school is moving towards achieving its aims.

Further Ideas

- Enhance the display with memorable or easily identifiable images of the school. In the example above, the school's house symbols – various birds – have been linked to the main school aims.

- Allow the children to contribute to the display by asking them to write their own aims for the school on the display as well. For the display above, children wrote their aims on feathers.

- Devise a school motto that underlines the main ethos, for example, 'Every day getting better in every way'. Display this in the hall so it is clearly visible to the whole school community.

- Create a school website that parents and pupils can access to obtain key information, such as term dates and forthcoming events.

- Set up an Internet café style point in school, accessible to children and parents who do not have a computer at home, to allow them to research and complete IT based homework.

Displays for Visitors

Communication with the wider school community can be a valuable opportunity to share aspects of school life. It can provide greater access and insight for visitors as well as draw their attention to matters that they may not necessarily be aware of. Creating a display to promote associations connected to the school, such as: 'The Friends of…' gives their efforts more prominence and acts as feedback on their activities. In this example, the display shows how fundraising for new playground equipment is progressing.

Display

1. Draw around a boy and a girl, lying down on cardboard to produce templates.

2. Cut each template in half down the middle of the body.

3. Using one half of each template, ask children to colour and add detail. Personalise the figures by painting them in the school uniform.

4. Mount the figures at either side of the display board.

5. From white card, cut out a simple thermometer shape as tall as the figures and mount it between them.

6. Add in detail, such as a blue or red strip down the middle of the thermometer with scale markings on both sides.

7. Make small arrows showing increasing monetary amounts, to stick on either side of the thermometer, leading to the target figure at the top.

8. From white card, cut out two thought bubbles to display the fundraising goal, and mount these above the figures of the children. Simply write in the bubbles or add children's drawings. Here, illustrations represent the goal of new playground equipment.

9. Use children's drawings or clip art to create images of money. These can be added to the thermometer as the funds grow. Create an eye-catching banner to top off the display.

Further Ideas

- Consider other points of entry for visitors to the school, especially those with younger children. Create a welcoming display for visitors to your classroom and use it to show key information about the work being taught in class, homework, and so on. Here, a colourful board for the Crocodile class features reminders for bringing in PE kit, and money for a zoo trip. It has been placed above a table with trays for delivery of homework and other books.

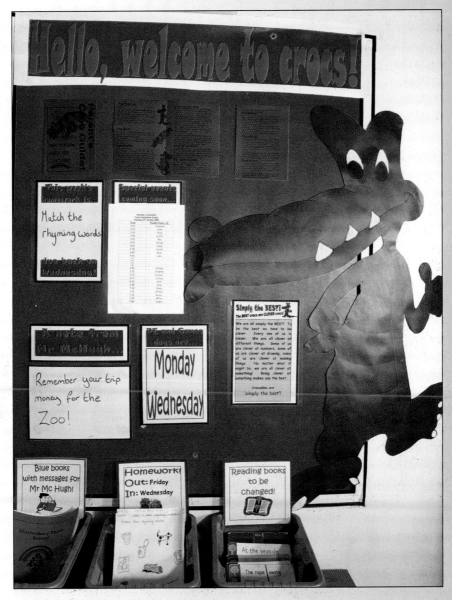

- Pin up current and past newsletters and reminders of forthcoming events.

- Fundraising targets can also be displayed to show the progress the school is making and where the money is being spent.

- This board could also be used to show notices from local companies, with the fee going towards the school funds. Similarly, people could be encouraged to post classified ads, again with the fee going towards the school.

- Photographs of past events or classroom activities can be put up to show people what is happening in your class or throughout the school.

School Community Displays

Providing a central information point for the wider school community encourages greater communication and stronger links with the school. Putting up a display that is essentially for parents and visitors to the school demonstrates that you value and acknowledge the part they can play in the school environment. It also is a great way to show pride in your school. A central contact point can become a window into the school and its classrooms, displaying its aims and ethos. It is also an opportunity for people to give feedback and suggestions, without being put on the spot by a questionnaire or a member of staff. A communication board could carry anything from photos of school events to copies of recent newsletters. In keeping with a whole school jungle theme, the display in this example has become a jungle hut, named 'The Jungle Telegraph'.

Display

1. Back the display board in green and edge with dark brown.

2. Cut out large leaf shaped templates to position around the border in bunches of three.

3. Make a canopy out of cardboard. Using one of the folds in a large box as a hinge, staple it to the top of the board and allow the cardboard to drop down to create the canopy.

4. Glue corrugated cardboard to the topside of the cardboard to give it more texture and paint it brown.

5. Pierce the two outside corners of the canopy with bamboo canes, long enough to reach the floor, as supports.

6. Use the bamboo to create vines. Attach small leaf shapes cut from green paper along the length of the 'vine', reversing the direction and position of the leaves as you go.

7. Cut three or four larger leaf shapes from a different coloured green paper. Attach them to brown border tape to trail across the canopy.

8. Create a banner to sit on the roof, for example: 'The Jungle Telegraph … Find out what we're about'.

9. Place a desk or table beneath the notice board, with a comments book to encourage parents to have their say: 'Have your 2p worth'. You may also want to provide a collection jar for coins.

- Compile individual leaflets or pocket guides to focus on different aspects of the school. The topics could range from different curriculum areas to school procedures and events planned for the year.

- Create an 'All about us' album. Keep pictures and local newspaper reports that feature the school in an album that is readily accessible and on display in the school reception. These clippings can be interspersed with the children's own write-ups and recollections of the events featured.

- Staff fact files can be a great way to introduce the different members of the school. Create a passport style page for each teacher. Include their general interests and information as well as comments from former pupils and other members of staff about the person pictured.

- Set up a display featuring the members of the governing body. This could show the different roles they have and what they become involved in. It could also show their progress and achievements for the current year.

Please feel free to take a Pocket Guide!

- Mount a display based on after-school activities. This could list the times and duration of each club and who is responsible, as well as carrying cancellation and other notices.

Early Years

The early years can often become isolated from the wider school community. Those entering this stage are generally too young to participate fully in many of the events designed for older children. However their contribution is just as valid, and it is important to create an environment in which they can feel relaxed, comfortable and part of the school. Here the early years have created a display with the aim of helping them settle into a new routine and identify themselves with the other children. The children have picked out key aspects of their day at school. This display can be used in a classroom as a constant visual reminder of the structure of the children's day. Alternatively, featured in a prominent position in school, it can act as a reminder to other children that there are new people in school who are not yet that confident about everything that happens in the day.

Display

1. Ask each child to create a self-portrait, using paint.

2. Cut out each portrait, mount on black paper and trim to match the shape of the picture, leaving a narrow black border.

3. Back the board in a strong colour that does not feature heavily in the children's paintings to help their faces stand out.

4. Add a border to match the mounting on the children's work.

5. Make a large clock face to fill half the board.

6. Add images in appropriate places on the clock to represent key times in the school day for the children (these can be created by the children).

7. Add labels that state in words what is happening at different times in the day.

8. Place the self-portraits around the clock and bursting out of the border.

9. Add banners to head the display, for example 'We are starting school' or 'Meet the Leopards' (class name).

Cross-curricular Links

- **Art:** get the children to create individual masks, linked to the whole school theme, to represent themselves. Here, the children have used fake fur fabric to cover mask templates and added details of wild animals in keeping with the school's jungle theme.

- **PSHCE:** set up a buddy system whereby the older children are linked to a child in early years. They can spend time reading and playing together at a specified time each week.

- **Art:** ask the children to paint portraits of children in other classes. Display the results and challenge the children to put names to the portraits.

- **Literacy:** children could create fact files about the school, themselves or even their 'buddy'.

- **General:** mount a display to show the type of equipment that the children in early years will be using for different activities.

- **Geography:** to familiarise the children with their new environment organise an information hunt around the school. This works in a similar way to a treasure hunt, but instead of clues the teacher asks questions, such as: 'Where do we find our reading books?'. The children then have to lead the teacher to the library. Questions can be posed for all the main areas in the school.

- **PSHCE:** allow the children to pose 'I know, I think, I wonder' questions about their new environment (see page 34).

Literacy Focus

Basing display on stories and books read in class is a great way to engage children's interest, especially in the early years. However, rather than just displaying images from the story, include key words and phrases from the text. The display can then act as a visual reminder and teaching aid during subsequent lessons. As a class, agree on the words and phrases you are going to use to describe characters or location. The initial framework for this can come from the story itself, with children identifying key words, and then extended through discussion. Challenge children to think of other describing words or to use at least, for example, three words from the display in their work. For the display shown here, the story of Three Billygoats Gruff has been used.

Display

1. Using an overhead projector, trace the outline of a photocopied image of a character onto a large sheet of paper.

2. Cut out the character and fill in the outline with a mixture of collage materials and paint. Use bright colours to make the character stand out and repeated layers of paper to add texture.

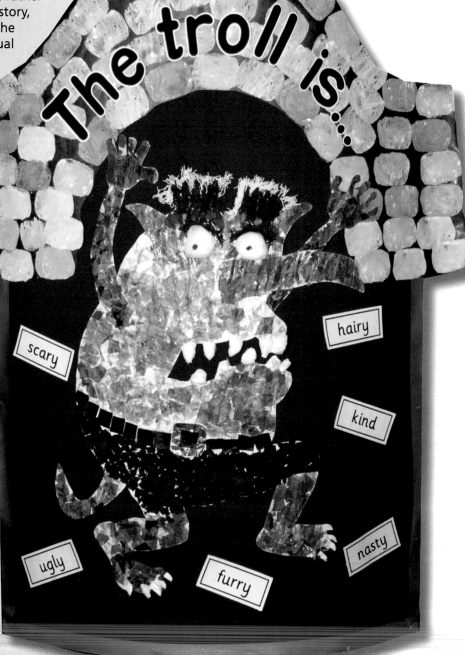

3. Create some of the scenery from the story to form the background for the display. Here, the children used sponge prints to depict bricks on a bridge template.

4. Paint or word process key words from the text that can be mounted and displayed with the images.

We read the story
'The Gingerbread Man' in Literacy.

Run, run as fast as you can

Cross-curricular Links

- **Art:** instead of one large image ask the children to create their own pictures of the main character in the story. This can be an effective way of engaging the children's interest in the story. In this example, the gingerbread men represent each child in the class. Key words could also be added. This can offer a challenge that operates on an individual level, where each child has to include their own key word(s) when talking or writing about the story.

- **Speaking and listening:** the class could participate in oral story telling based on the story they are studying. Each child suggests one line of the story as you move around the class. However, each sentence must start with, or include a key word shown on the board.

- **Literacy:** you could mount multiple displays in the classroom, depicting various traditional stories. Link the displays with a path or 'yellow brick road'. Devise a class character that can be displayed in each scene and moved around as the class studies the different stories.

- **Design and Technology:** children could make a mask of a character from the stories as well as their clothes. Then you could stage a themed day when the children come to school dressed as a character from a traditional story.

- **Design and Technology:** organise the children into groups and give each group a different traditional story as inspiration for a 3D model. They could produce characters as well as a background scene and use them to retell the story.

Science Focus

Studying artists and their work is a great way to expose children to different styles and media in art. It is worth remembering that using different artists' pictures does not mean you have to produce a replica of their work. The cogs and wheels display in the example is an excellent use of printing, but its inspiration could have come from the erratic style of Jackson Pollock or the printed patterns of William Morris. Furthermore, if the art lesson is following a certain skill, technique or medium then any outcome with the final piece of work is acceptable. This can be especially advantageous when considering possible cross-curricular activities. The caterpillar display on page 57 not only involved the children in colour mixing in Art, but also linked to their mini beast topic in Science.

Display

1. Look at various pictures and images of the artist the class is studying.

2. Create different patterns using a variety of materials from paint to pastels.

3. Collect together a number of objects that can be used for printing. In this example, the class has focused on cogs and wheels.

4. Let the children experiment, using these objects to print onto paper. They can either print an image face down, or run the wheels or cogs across the page.

5. Mount the work in an erratic fashion to reflect the artist's style, thereby creating one large piece of printing, as the gaps between each piece of work become almost incidental when viewed from a distance. Here, using a corner of the room creates an effective display.

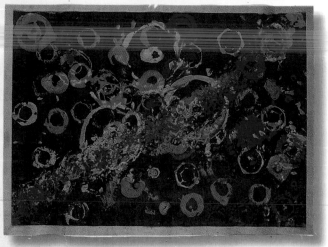

56

Cross-curricular Links

- **Design and Technology:** link the cogs artwork to a project based on moving vehicles, where the children will be experimenting with wheels and camshafts when building their own 3D model of a car.

- **Numeracy:** look at the style of the artist Seurat. Rather than using dots (circles) to create a picture allow the children to choose any 2D shape to create their composition.

- **Science/Design and Technology:** make 3D models of insects from their science topic. Use different artists' styles to show various ways in which detail can be added. For example, look at the shapes and bright colours used by David McKee in his illustrations of Elmer the elephant (published by Red Fox).

- **Literacy:** use an abstract artwork as a basis for discussion in class. Ask the children what they can see in the chosen picture. Can anyone describe any objects they see in the picture? Challenge the children to use a copy of the picture as a backdrop and draw in the objects they have described.

History Focus

Introducing a cross-curricular element into lessons does not necessarily mean relying on a connecting or similar feature. In this example, a history topic about Florence Nightingale has been carried into an art lesson. The main skill of the lesson is based on using 'hot' and 'cold' colours and geometric shapes to create a portrait. However, the image of Florence Nightingale has been used to demonstrate facial features and as a subject for their artwork. This lesson would have worked quite successfully without the Florence Nightingale connection, but this way, her image is repeatedly reinforced. It also allows some cross-referencing to occur in the lesson, by the teacher just double-checking who she was, what she did and where, and so on.

Display

1. Find an image of Paul Klee's *Senecio (The Face)* for reference. Challenge the children to create a portrait, just using geometric shapes to form the facial features.

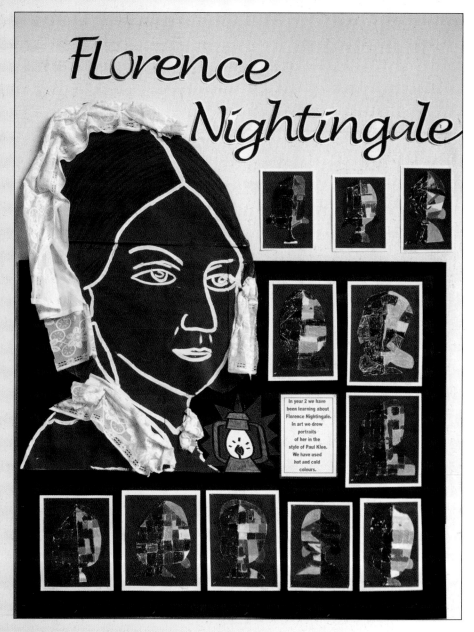

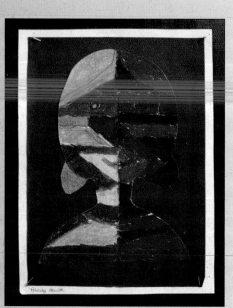

2. Ask the children to draw a dividing line cutting their pictures into two, down the middle of the face. Get them to colour the different shapes on one side in 'hot' colours, such as red, yellow and orange, and the other in 'cold' colours (shades of blue, green and white). They could use various media, but pastel on black sugar paper is effective.

3. Cut out the portraits and double mount them on black then white backgrounds.

4. Back the board in a strong colour.

5. Photocopy an image of Florence onto acetate, and using an overhead projector, trace the image onto black paper.

6. Cut out the silhouette outline of Florence. Use white paint for her facial features. Add white netting for her shawl for a tactile quality.

7. Mount the work using the 'Box' and 'Vertical' methods (shown on page 72) to create a neat visual display.

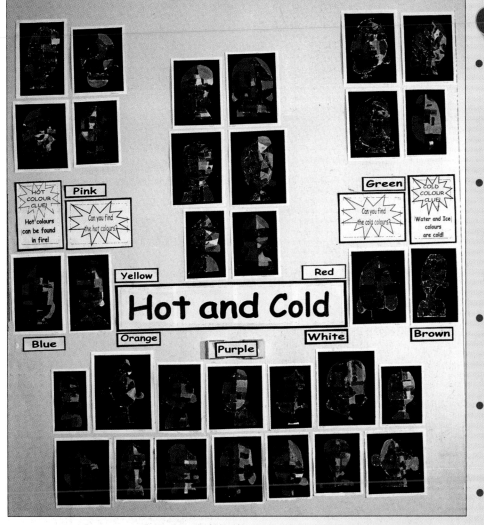

HOT COLOUR CLUE! Hot colours can be found in fire!

Pink — Can you find the hot colours?

Green

Can you find the cold colours?

COLD COLOUR CLUE! Water and Ice colours are cold!

Yellow

Red

Hot and Cold

Blue

Orange

Purple

White

Brown

- **Literacy:** ask the children to imagine they are Florence Nightingale, and to write a letter home about the experiences she has faced. (These can be 'aged', using tea bags, to create a separate display.)

- **Drama:** hot seating. Ask a succession of children to take on the role of Florence and empathise with her situation by responding to questions from the class. Alternatively, ask a parent helper to come in and 'act' the role of Florence.

- **Science/PSHCE:** draw the children's attention to the conditions faced by Florence in her hospital and link this to healthy living schemes of work.

- **Literacy:** suggest the children maintain a diary or journal like Florence. They could keep a daily journal, which they could compare with Florence's.

- **Drama:** role play. Challenge the children to re-enact Florence's arrival at the hospital and to voice her concerns about the conditions she faced.

- **Geography:** locate on a map where Florence was working and discuss its position in relation to Britain. Spend some time thinking about how Florence would have travelled there.

Dear...

Love Florence xx

Ancient Greece

Sticking to a rigid structure of set lessons on set topics can become as monotonous for the children as for the teachers. Working on topics that extend across other curriculum areas and alter the normal timetable can revitalise a child's interest or present a topic in a different light. Studying the Ancient Greeks is an ideal example of how cross-curricular activities can take place under the umbrella of one theme. The topic transfers easily to other subject areas and consequently becomes accessible to more children. It also offers an opportunity for cross-curricular display, when samples of work from each subject can be brought together in one setting. Making large 3D structures to represent Greek columns is an eye-catching way of dividing the board into sections for the various pieces of work.

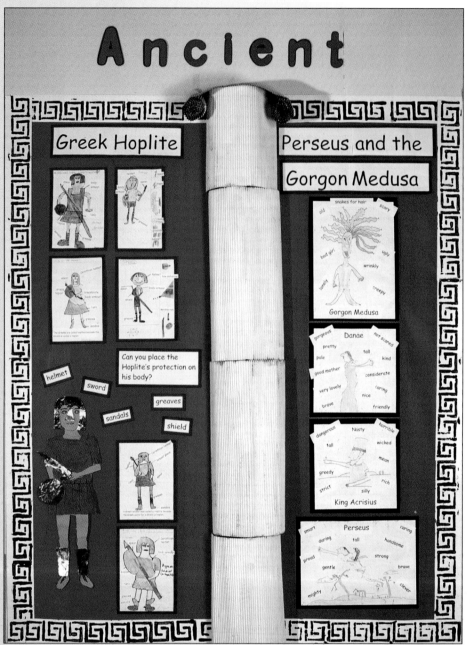

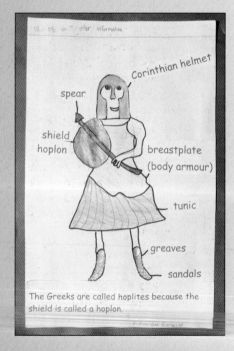

Display

1. Have the children create a border for the display, using a repeating pattern design similar to those found in Ancient Greek artwork.

2. Back the board in a light yellow or orange backing paper to give the impression of sandstone. If possible, using a spray-mount glue, stick some sand over the backing paper to add texture.

3. Divide the board down the middle with a large Greek column. Use corrugated cardboard, painted in an off white colour. Staple one edge of the cardboard and bend round to form a curve and staple the other edge to the board. Stuff the middle with newspaper to bolster the corrugated cardboard and retain the 3D effect. Work in segments until the column runs the full height of the board (where possible down to the floor).

4. Across the top of the column lay a strip of corrugated cardboard with the edges curled into rolls on either side.

5. Display on the board a variety of work, covering different areas of the curriculum.

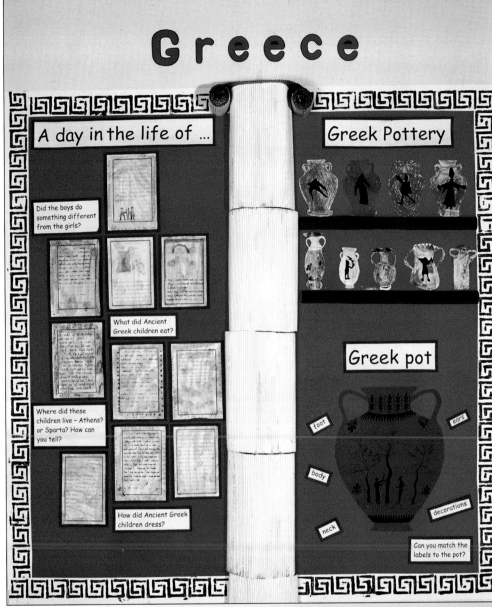

Cross-curricular Links

- **Art:** look at the repeating patterns used in Ancient Greek art and architecture.

- **Numeracy:** continue the study of the patterns and link it to symmetry.

- **Art:** use patterns and images to create 2D Greek pots. Incorporate some of the patterns from the other sessions.

- **Design and Technology:** use the designs discovered in the art lessons to make 3D clay models of Greek pots.

- **Literacy:** study the myths of Ancient Greece and ask the children to create their own stories and mythical monsters.

- **Literacy:** encourage the children to empathise with the daily lives of the Ancient Greek people and ask them to write a diary or account of a day in the life of an Ancient Greek.

- **Design and Technology:** look at the architecture of Ancient Greece and organise the children into small groups to make Greek buildings. Paint the structures white and add details using pattern.

- **Drama/PE:** hold an Ancient Greek day when the children can dress as Ancient Greeks and experience typical food of the period and activities through the day. (See page 70.)

RE Focus

It is stimulating to study different cultures and beliefs and it is possible to link that study across several curriculum areas. Aboriginal art is simplistic and makes use of simple lines and repeated patterns. The symbolism and beliefs that lay behind their art and dreamtime stories can be explored in other lessons as well. Looking at other cultures allows children to feel that they can contribute information about their own backgrounds more easily. Allowing this study to continue outside RE and PSHCE lessons ensures a greater exposure for the children and therefore more opportunities for them to express themselves.

Display

1. Back the board in light orange in order to highlight the black silhouettes.

2. Look at examples of Aboriginal art and ask the children to choose an animal. Tell them they are only to draw a 2D shape from above or in profile (side on) to keep within the correct style.

3. Cut out the animal shapes and place them on black sugar paper as a template.

4. Give the children cotton buds and ask them to place dots of paint in a single colour around the outside of their animal template.

5. This is repeated using different colours in growing rings around the template. The children should initially be restricted to colours found in Aboriginal art (red, white and yellow). They should repeat these colours in the same order until they run out of space.

6. Remove the template to reveal the Aboriginal art. Cut off the sharp edges and unused parts of the black sugar paper. The space where the template has been is normally left blank, but can be decorated with Aboriginal patterns using pastels.

7. Display the animals as if moving across the board. Add in extra details, such as plants and rocks, to give an idea of the environment, along with quotes from Aboriginal dreamtime stories.

Cross-curricular Links

- **Art:** challenge the children to create a symbol or image to represent themselves and record those images onto palm-sized pebbles. Use the cotton bud technique explained on page 62, but allow them to experiment with different colours. Using pebbles is a great way for the children to make something to keep. (If they make a mistake the pebble easily washes clean. Once complete, varnish the pebble to preserve the work.)

- **Art:** look at the symbolism involved in Aboriginal art. Can the children devise images or symbols from their own lives? Perhaps they could draw their journey to school in Aboriginal style.

- **Geography:** compare and contrast the environment where Aboriginal people live to where the school is situated.

- **RE/Art:** read and discuss the meaning of Aboriginal dreamtime stories. Can the children convert a simple story into a series of pictures and symbols?

- **Literacy:** can the children write a dreamtime story based on examples of Aboriginal art?

- **Drama:** act out the Aboriginal story of creation.

- **RE:** discuss Aboriginal beliefs. Compare their beliefs with those from other cultures and religions. Create a display that features images and beliefs from different cultures. Use work and writing from different age groups across the school to represent a wide variety of beliefs from the cultures the different year groups study.

- **Geography:** compare Aboriginal dreamtime art and stories with those of other indigenous peoples, for example, Native Americans and their use of dream catchers. Children could make their own dream catchers for a colourful display.

Geography Focus

Quite often teachers repeat the same topics every year and, as a consequence, it is tempting to re-create the same displays each time. While this obviously ensures some ease in creating a display, it is possible for the lessons to become tailored to that idea and therefore grow stale. Changing the display can often lead to new insights to a text. The key is to be creative and different in your approach. In the example used here as part of a geography topic, five main

The usual suspects of the Isle of Struay

Mrs McColl   Neilly Beag   Granma Mainland   Grannie Island

Katie Morag

characters from the Katie Morag stories (by Mairi Hedderwick, published by Red Fox) have been displayed as the 'usual suspects' in a line-up. Showing the characters as silhouettes presents them as slightly sinister or indistinct and immediately the children begin to identify and name them. The class could then be challenged to create fact files about the 'suspects' or create new silhouettes (new characters) or even storylines for the scenario on display. While the display is not a scene from a story, it is easy to relate it to the text. Approaching display from a different angle can open up many new ideas in the classroom.

Neilly Beag

Display

1. Back the board in a brilliant white. (Tip: the back of some backing paper can be used if you do not have a white roll.)

2. Using thin black edging tape, create lines across at regular intervals, 30cm apart.

3. Draw the key characters from the text onto acetate, enlarged to about three-quarters of A4 size.

4. Using an overhead projector, trace the outline of the characters onto black sugar paper. The figures need to be large enough to fill the background of the board.

5. Identify a common feature in each character and re-create this in colour to help them become more readily recognisable. In this example, each character's hat or hairstyle has been coloured. (When you have finished tracing the outline of the character, replace the paper with a coloured sheet and trace the hat or hair.)

6. Cut out the hat or hair, finish by drawing on details and stick into position on the correct silhouette.

7. Label each character with their name in a strong colour to stand out on the black and white setting.

8. Mount the children's brightly coloured work on and around the silhouettes.

Cross-curricular Links

- **Literacy:** challenge the children to create their own character or storyline.

- **Literacy:** ask the children to compile a character fact file using several texts or stories to build their knowledge.

- **Design and Technology:** build a model of the environment in which the story is set – in the case of Katie Morag it is an island. Children could make different models of the characters' houses.

- **Science:** make a simple circuit to light a bulb for a model of the lighthouse featured in the Katie Morag stories.

- **Geography:** split the class and set half to creating a brochure about the island and the other half a brochure about the mainland. Compare and contrast the finished brochures.

Katie Morag

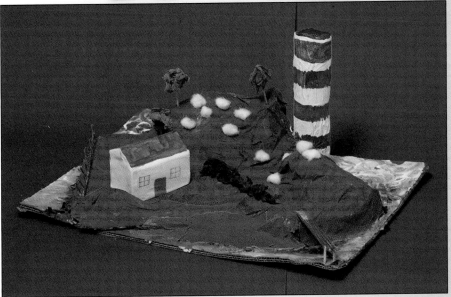

- **Geography:** discuss the environment on the island and the clothes the characters wear. Compare this to another location.

- **ICT:** swap emails with a school in another location.

- **Design and Technology:** look at the different ways in which you could reach the island in the Katie Morag stories. Challenge the children to construct a bridge that could hold a small weight, such as a toy car.

Choosing a Theme

Increasingly, schools are using themed weeks to deliver a wide variety of experiences and ideas in the classroom. Furthermore, applying the theme on a school-wide basis creates an exciting buzz throughout the age groups. Challenging teachers to devise a range of activities based on a central concept stimulates their teaching as well as the children's imagination. Art is the most readily accessible subject to tie in with a themed idea. However, the resulting work can be used to extend experiences and activities within other curriculum areas as well. The examples shown here have come from a school using a carnival theme. The older children were able to do some direct work based on the idea of carnival masks, while younger children looked at a circus.

Display

1. Make individual carnival masks with modroc. Apply a thin layer of petroleum jelly to the children's faces, especially to the eyebrows, to ensure easy removal of the masks. Build up layers of modroc on their faces to create the mask. Remove the masks carefully once dry. Parental consent is required for this activity.

2. Encourage them to think about the completed design beforehand, so they can add the required shapes to their masks; for example, the sun mask shown (left) is fringed with 'flames'.

3. Once dry, allow the children to paint designs onto their masks.

4. Back the display board in a dark colour to help show off the masks.

5. Using black backing paper, create a large eye mask shape to mount across the top of the board.

6. Cut feather shapes from paper in various bright colours to form the top part of the eye mask.

7. Edge the mask in a gold trim to make it stand out from the board.

8. Mount the individual masks beneath the large eye mask, using small pins or nails.

Cross-curricular Links

- **Art:** younger children may not have as great an understanding of a carnival as older children. However, most will be aware of a circus and can relate to the idea of an organised spectacle. Let the children create their own clown masks using screwed up tissue paper glued down to make the facial features. These could be displayed along with a circus tent.

- **Art:** face painting activities could be offered to the younger children, while older children can come up with their own designs. Parental consent is advisable for this activity, in case of allergic reactions.

- **PE:** children could work on the movements and display of a carnival or circus parade. They could work in set balances, with children holding a pose for a few seconds or controlled movements. They could even have a juggling master class or put a little show together to perform at the end of the day. The display here incorporated photographs of children practising circus skills.

- **Literacy:** ask the children to produce a creative writing piece about the sights and sounds of the carnival as it passes them by or what it is like to be a carnival dancer. Alternatively, they could write about a trip to the circus.

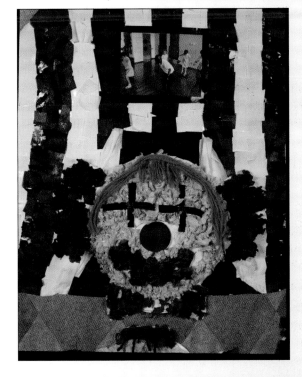

- **Geography/RE/PSHCE:** look at the different carnivals and festivals that are held around the world and the ways in which they are celebrated.

- **Art/Design and Technology:** children could work on creating carnival or circus costumes using chicken wire to build a wearable frame that could then be brightly decorated.

Art Theme

Use the work of famous artists as a basis for your school's theme. Decide on a single artwork, then devise a variety of linked activities that can take place in each year group, throughout the school. This is a great opportunity for children to become more familiar with different works of art, and to give them a greater awareness of the vast scope of paintings that are available, rather than relying on the usual famous pieces. It is also a good strategy for teachers to use as a different stimulus to introduce lessons. Children can be asked to suggest the story behind a painting, and discuss what might have been happening just before the scene was painted. In a maths lesson they could be asked to identify any shapes they can see. In this example, the school has chosen to reproduce figures from a famous painting, *The Marquise de Seignelay and Two of her Sons*, by Pierre Mignard, as one of their activities.

Display

1. Look at the figure(s) in your chosen painting and get children to practise drawing the figure(s) and the composition in their sketchbooks. Children could even practise modelling the pose(s) in the classroom.

2. From cardboard, cut out life-sized templates of the figure(s) in the picture.

3. Working in small groups, ask the children to focus on a small section of the figure(s) and add colour and detail using collage materials and overlapping small pieces of paper. Supply a wide variety of a material to provide rich detail for the collage, for example, fabrics, card, tissue, crêpe and coloured paper.

Cross-curricular Links

- **Art:** using papier-mâché, build up layers to create a 3D effect on your reproduction. Make various appendages of the figure(s) stand out from the flat surface, as if the character is coming to life out of the painting, such as the blue cloth on the figure shown on page 68. Another idea is to re-create the scene by painting a background and adding photographs cut from magazines. You can also try different compositions as shown here.

- **Art:** work on a smaller scale to reproduce an entire picture including the frame, in the example shown here, (left), the work was based on *Self-portrait in a Straw Hat* by Marie Louise Elisabeth Vigée-le-Brun. Use a mixture of paint and collage materials to reproduce the background and add detail. Over time the different pieces can build up to produce a famous picture gallery.

- **Drama:** look at what is happening in your chosen painting. Ask the children to dress up as the characters and stage a scene to explain the events going on in the picture. Alternatively, you could challenge the children to write a scene of a play based on the painting.

- **Geography:** use landscape paintings to identify different types of environment. Ask the children to continue the landscapes to the immediate left or right of the picture. In the example below, seascapes rather than landscapes provided inspiration. The children could either maintain a similar environment or drastically change it. Take ideas from your local surroundings.

- **History:** treat paintings as a historical source. Ask what can this painting tell us about the period in which it was painted? Look at the way the people are dressed, how they lived and even what they ate. Consider whether it is a reliable, historical source or whether the painter was biased.

Theme Days

Using a theme across a school can be really effective in generating a fantastic range of activities and displays all based on the same concept. Allowing the children in each age group to work on the same idea(s) can create a great atmosphere, which is enhanced by the dedication of an entire day to activities connected to the theme. The theme in question does not necessarily have to be linked to the curriculum or any particular social event. In the example used here, the school adopted a theme of Dragon Day (which could readily be linked to St George's Day). Other ideas include an 'artist's day' when each class in the school focuses on a particular artist and participates in activities based on their work.

Display

1. Create a large dragon face out of cardboard.

2. Allow the children in the class to help paint the face. Children could be given the responsibility to colour in individual scales.

3. Mount the face on the wall and add green netting or fabric to suggest the dragon's body.

4. Create a flame template and cut out plenty of flames from black sugar paper. Ask each child to colour in a flame with chalk pastels.

5. Position the flames on the wall, spreading outwards from the dragon's head to give the impression that it is breathing fire.

6. Use the flames to act as individual mountings for related work.

Cross-curricular Links

- **Drama/Literacy:** write a play about a dragon with your class. Pick a simple theme and through class discussion, devise a script. This could be performed as an assembly.

- **Art:** create an individual dragon mask for each member of the class. These could be used in your play.

- **Literacy:** ask your class to create an advertisement or poster entitled 'Dragon for hire'. Discuss the different activities your dragon could be hired out for – from crushing armies to mowing the lawn and cooking Sunday dinner!

- **Art:** make clay dragons. Create a long, sinuous body before attaching legs and wings. Paint them in bright colours and name them.

Artist's Day

When studying an artist, do not always settle for painting an individual replica of their work. In this example, the school held a Picasso day. Their display shows portraits with distorted faces in typical Picasso style.

Display

1. Ask the children to paint a self-portrait in the style of Picasso. Cut up a rectangular piece of mirrored card, as though it had been shattered. Mount the pieces onto black sugar paper, slightly apart from each other, but maintaining the rectangular shape. Trim the sugar paper, leaving a border.

2. By looking at themselves in this 'mirror' children can see their own distorted faces and gain insight into how to tackle their portrait.

3. Encourage them to add features in odd places and divide the face into irregular shapes with bold colours.

4. Mount the portraits on different coloured paper and display with the 'shattered' mirror.

Cross-curricular Links

- **Literacy:** challenge the children to write a description of some of Picasso's portraits. Emphasise that they should try to talk about the strange positioning of the features. To make it more exciting and accessible tell them to imagine that they have just met a stranger in a dark alley who looks like a Picasso portrait and ask them to describe him.

- **Art:** create a massive homage to an artist whereby each child contributes to one big picture. In this example, the children studied the work of Kandinsky. Using geometrical shapes they have created a class piece in the style of Kandinsky.

Art in the style of Kandinsky

Display Methods

Combining work of various sizes need not be problematical when creating a display. There are various methods you can use effectively to enable you to exhibit a wide range of work in an individual display. These methods work best when displaying square mounted work but can also be applied to irregular shaped pieces as well.

Display Techniques

- **Box:** for displaying work where the outside edges of the pieces form a box shape. It is ideal for rectangular or square pieces of work, as long as the outer edges create the box then the display retains a sense of order, even with large spaces in between. The Flower Power display above is a good example of this. Here, the children have created 3D flowers that stand out from the page. The work is displayed in both portrait and landscape positions using the box method. The work is positioned so that the edges of various pieces clearly form a corner shape. This is repeated so that when looking at the whole board they suggest an outline box shape. This way the overall effect appears more organised.

- **Cross:** displaying work around a centrally located cross which is created by the individual work edges. The cross can dominate the centre of the board or several small crosses can be created around a board. The Emotions display on page 26 has a large cross formed by the artwork running through the centre of the board.

- **Horizontal/Vertical:** these are ideal to use on very long or very tall boards. Areas in schools where these prove successful are corridors and halls. Work of varying sizes can be mounted as long as one edge of each piece is mounted in line with the next. Displaying time lines in this manner is very effective and allows for a range of work to be shown. The Florence Nightingale display on page 58 is a good example of this method.